GOLDEN TONES: WRITING WITH SOUL

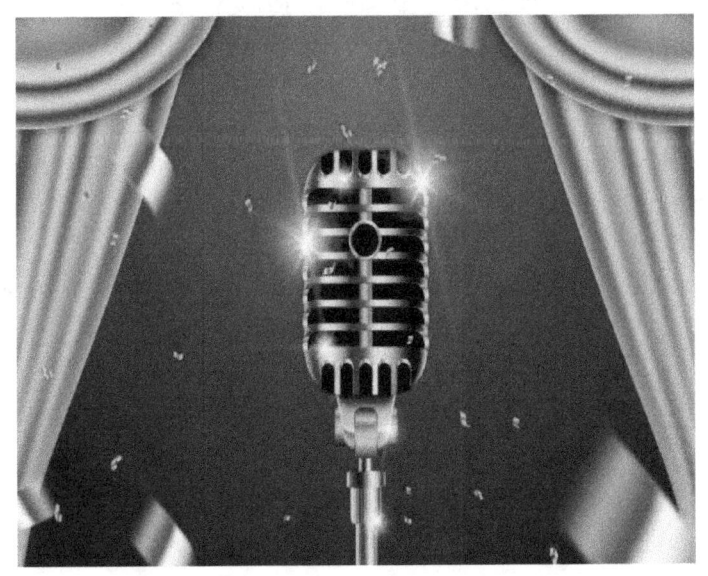

Real Talk About Real Life Things

By

Chelsea G. Robinson

GOLDEN TONES:
WRITING WITH SOUL

© 2019. Chelsea G. Robinson
ISBN: 9781090245441

All Rights Reserved.
No part of this book may be reproduced or transmitted in any form or by any means, electronic or mechanical, including photocopying and recording, or by any information storage and retrieval system, without permission from the publisher.

FOREWORD

Raw! Riveting! Real! These words describe what you will experience as you thumb through the pages of Golden Tones: Writing with Soul . . . Real Talk About Real Life Things. Chelsea expresses how she, as a strong African American Woman, feels about everything . . . from being a person who is curious to touch a black woman's hair to dealing with such subjects as grief, death, and dying. She writes about her truths with an upbeat flow of rhythm and rhyme.

I have known Chelsea for nearly 10 years and I'm honored to write this Foreword. She is well on her way to becoming a recognized and celebrated author and poet. Just as an instrument plays the notes to a melody, her convictions dance off the page--flowing, precise, and captivating. As a composer arranges his music score, Chelsea has meticulously arranged some of her best work in this beautiful collection of poems.

There's no hesitation on her part. Chelsea boldly declares how grandmothers influence the lives of the people around them. And supported by Biblical scriptures, Chelsea writes about friendships and relationships. Chelsea leaves no stone unturned as she addresses many important issues such as domestic violence, young love, and even police brutality. This collection, as her first published work, is quite impressive and you are sure to find yourself, as I did, caught up in her writings--even seeing yourself through the eyes of this brutally honest and wonderfully talented new writer, Chelsea G. Robinson.

Respectfully Submitted,
Andrea Dudley, CEO
Habakkuk Publishing

DEDICATION

This book is dedicated to my family and close friends as well as my <u>Oral Interpretation of Literature</u> instructor, Carol Bennett.

Also, a special "Thank You" to everyone who has supported me during this journey.

I hope all of you enjoy this book.

Best –
Chelsea G. Robinson

INTRODUCTION:

Setting The Stage . . .

You feel like your voice has been lost in the madness of your everyday life and you just want to be heard. It feels like you have been fighting barriers and obstacles on a regular basis and wonder: "Does anybody understand what I'm going through?"

Close your eyes. . .

Let your mind relax and picture a small, cozy bistro filled with dozens of chairs for the audience. However, as your mind relaxes, you realize there is a special chair reserved just for you. . . .

. . . and you sit.

As the lights dim around you, a golden glow lights up the stage. As you watch, the golden spotlight falls upon a single microphone in the middle of the stage and the soothing sounds of smooth jazz envelop you.

Keep these images in your mind as you read this book, a poetic affirmation created just for you and know that you have been heard.

Your life **does** have meaning.

TABLE OF CONTENTS

Foreword iii
Dedication iv
Introduction: v
Unapologetically Me 3
My First Heartbreak 7
Don't Touch My Hair 11
Baa, Baa Black And Fabulous Sheep 15
Speak Up! 19
Police Brutality 21
Old School Love 25
What's A Role Model? 27
Don't Fight The Side Chick 31
Black Lives Matter? 35
Live Your Best Life 39
Allow Inspiration 41
Teenage Girl 43
Grief 47
Church Hurt 51
Real Love 55
Grandma's Hands: For Omealia 59
Mama's Heart 61
Just One More Drink 63
Better 67
Blue Skies 71
It Was A One Time Thing 73

Jesus	77
Good Vibez Only	79
A Friend	83
Rough And Tough Addictions	87
Rejection	91
I Got Some Candy!	93
No Real Commitment	97
One Day Child	101
School Educated Me	105
Be That One Light	109
Gossip Bug	111
"Soul Sistah"	113
Team Natural	117
By The Lockers	119
Late	123
If You Gave Up Today	127
Fear	131
Abortion	135
Before U Approach Me	139
To Pac . . .	143
Failure	147
Losing You	151
To Florene	155
Reconciliation	159
Young 'N Broke	163
Poverty Line	167
Dear Little Chelsea	169
Father Famine	173
Comparison Is A Toxin	177
Author Biography	179

Chelsea G. Robinson

READER'S NOTES . . .

1 Corinthians 15:10 "But by the grace of God I am what I am, and his grace toward me was not in vain. On the contrary, I worked harder than any of them, though it was not I, but the grace of God that is with me."

UNAPOLOGETICALLY ME

1 Corinthians 15:10

I like to live on my own terms. Yeah, you guessed it. I've always been like this; from the womb, if you will! I don't like being told *what* to do, *who* to love, *how* to act, *how* to dress, *how* to speak! I have my own brain! I'm NO one's scarecrow!

This is my story; this is ME! Unapologetically, ME! I don't just dance to the beat of my own drum.

I AM THE DANCE! I AM THE BEAT! I AM THE DRUM!

So many times, people have tried to dumb me down; tried to silence me, tried to get me to be like the rest! I allowed it for a minute, and I blended in just like the perfect shade of concealer on a woman's skin!

AND I HATED IT!

I'm even guilty of doing the things I listed above, to my own self. But I always come to the same conclusion. Over and over "one more 'gain!

Why should I try so hard to fit in when The Good Lord created me in a custom-made fashion?

I was born to do me! With that being said, I'm my own woman! I may even fall and fail sometimes. But I always manage to GET

BACK UP! And I do it my way, once again.

I am a survivor, an overcomer, a victor! Take time to see ME, to hear me out! Now this is a word to my haters, doubters, and all the naysayers of America. . .

I. AM. ME.

READER'S NOTES . . .

Romans 3:3 "What if some were unfaithful? Does their faithlessness nullify the faithfulness of God?"

MY FIRST HEARTBREAK

Romans 3:3

Do you remember all those times? Yeah, the ones where you stood me up?

Each and every time, there just happened to be a brand new lie. How stupid can I be?

To think: "Maybe he'll come through this time."

There was one time. Yeah. ONE single time that you actually came through in the clutch.

I never thought there would be so much lust. Yep. Lust and dreams. You had me going for a minute. Had me thinking we were some dream team. You meant the world to me, I quickly made you my everything, including the very song I'd sing,

Then you became different. I wish I had a catalog of all of the things you did to me.

Even if that was granted to me, I probably wouldn't have had the eyes to see how much you truly failed to love me . . .

I cried, and prayed.

I prayed and cried.

The more God ripped us apart, the more I tried to hide.

Never understood how the person I wanted since fourth grade could cause such a charade.

I felt so betrayed.

I never got how you never could truly feel me.

Now I understand and see. . . .

        You just weren't made for my destiny.

READER'S NOTES . . .

Psalm 104:9 "You set a boundary that they may not pass, so that they might not again cover the earth."

DON'T TOUCH MY HAIR

Psalm 104:9

What goes through your mind when you tug at my coils?

Spoiler Alert:

I HATE WHEN YOU DO THAT!!

You can't just come up and pet me like I'm some cat!

And then you have the nerve to insult my kitchen!

Listen, I don't care to hear that you'll be darker than me this summer after you've sat on top of your Jeep or Hummer for ten hours!

I don't care about how much you think the black guy next door is hot, and no, I'm not his cousin!

Black people are not all the same, we come a dime a dozen!

I don't want to watch "Frozen."

I don't know why I was chosen - by YOU - to be "National Spokesperson For Black Folks Of America!"

No, I don't want to braid your hair, and "No" you still can't touch mine!

Respect my space. Be courteous and kind, and we won't have any issues. As a matter of fact, we will be just fine!

Oh! Now look, here you go! Reaching for my hair again! My face probably reads "DO YOU MIND?"

Fatha! Lawd Jesus, open the eyes of the blind! I'm starting to think my soap box lectures are just a waste of time! Would you like it if I did that to you? Oh you don't care? WELL I DO! So back away! Way, way far away; a lifetime away from me!

I'm sick of being treated like my kind is still property. It's more and deeper than you touching my hair.

      It's obnoxious that I even had to take it there.

READER'S NOTES . . .

Psalm 46:5 "God is in the midst of her; she shall not be moved: God shall help her, and that right early."

BAA, BAA BLACK AND FABULOUS SHEEP

Psalm 46:5

Being the black sheep of my family; I can say I like it! If you haven't noticed, black is slimming; it's okay to be different!

But as for me? No, I'm not timid.

As many already know, I am what I am. There's no pretending, there's no show!

I may not fit into y'all's "American Dream" and all that! But I'm not one to fake, make no mistake!

Furthermore, I won't bend for anyone!

Yep you guessed it, I WILL NOT BREAK!

I will still do whatever it takes to make the name great!

For as long as I live, I'll be myself. God didn't need any help when making me the girl that I am.

Why should I pretend that my personality and all that I naturally have is a sham?

I will never shut up! I will never be quiet! Nothing that you could possibly throw at me will dissolve my dignity!

I'm really not the enemy, I'm just me. I won't change who I am, just so you can be happy and at ease!

And if you thought I would; Girl, Please! Respect the beast in me! Say whatever to make yourself feel better!

But I still believe in ME!

READER'S NOTES . . .

Isaiah 58:1 "Cry aloud; do not hold back; lift up your voice like a trumpet, declare to my people their transgression, to the house of Jacob their sins."

SPEAK UP!

Isaiah 58:1

Y ou, My Friend, have a voice.

You, My Friend, have a choice to use that voice.

Don't be scared now, be nice and loud! Make some noise!

Some may not like it; they can full on detest it! They may look at you crazy!

Their eyes can water! You have to be a finisher, since you're a starter!

Begin to tell us how you really feel!

I'm here for the drama; I'm here for the chills. I may even be here cheering you on, right next to your mama!

Don't let them get you down, so what? You've seen a few frowns?

I'd rather you speak your peace than to see you drown and fall to your knees!

In case you feel a bit of unease, remember the 'realest of the real' sees you as the bees' knees!

Be daring, be you!

> Be everything you are and say everything
> you were born to!

READER'S NOTES . . .

Jeremiah 22:3 "Thus says the Lord: Do justice and righteousness and deliver from the hand of the oppressor him who has been robbed. And do no wrong or violence to the resident alien, the fatherless, and the widow, nor shed innocent blood in this place."

POLICE BRUTALITY

Jeremiah 22:3

It was a mistake?

Is that the best excuse you could conjure up?

It was an accident? Really? Okay?

Now tell me somethin': why do ya'll mistake folks having a weapon, and it's just a phone, but when a shrimp boy with porcelain skin is actually a killer, you barely touch him?

Goes to show you can't do jack while being black! That is, without being attacked.

Yeah you've got the idea... No Skittles!™ No Arizona Tea!™ No selling cigarettes or CDs!

No fail to turn signals, can't even chill in your own yard!

It's a hot mess and ya know it. It wouldn't hurt you none if you showed it! Show that you aren't the foolish folks we think you are!

You kill a black person for no reason then get paid time off, and parade around like you're some "Movie Star!"

If it were up to me, most of ya'll would be jobless! You can find another career, but the victims' families' won't ever be able to find another kid!

This thing called life ain't replaceable, I just wish ya'll knew your place and all!

Your job is to SERVE but instead. . .

>You have a God complex and it's truly wrecking my nerves!

READER'S NOTES . . .

John 15:9 "As the Father has loved me, so have I loved you. Abide in my love."

Genesis 2:18 Then the Lord God said, "It is not good that the man should be alone; I will make him a helper fit for him."

OLD SCHOOL LOVE

John 15:9 Genesis 2:18

If it don't feel like old school rhythm and blues, I don't want it.

If the loving vibe don't remind me of a song by Smokey, I will drop it!

Show me a man who ain't afraid to cry for his woman like David Ruffin and maybe, just maybe, you'll be tellin' me something!

Give me that kind of love where no matter how far we may have to travel away from each other, we will always be reunited.

Just like the "Voyage to Atlantis."

That's the love I want.

I want someone that makes me feel like I'm on the "Stairway to Heaven" every time we meet.

I'ma g'on get me a man who says: "You are everything, and everything is you."

And when I finally do get him, I can confidently promise you that if it came down to me being with him, or being happy....

I wouldn't have to choose.

READER'S NOTES . . .

Proverbs 22:1 "A good name is to be chosen rather than great riches and favor is better than silver or gold."

WHAT'S A ROLE MODEL?

Proverbs 22:1

Nowadays. . .

Real. Raw. Authentic talent is overlooked.

While "THOT"-fulness, ratchedness, and carrying on will get you overbooked!

No morals, no values, no originality.

Ya'll paying for these females' houses, but they all have the same personality!

Oh, another piece of advice for the next up and coming IT girl. . .

Make sure your body from the waist down is shaped like a wisdom tooth!

Instead of going to school, building heart and character, and blossoming into something beautiful.

Get injections in your thighs to match your behind, and despise your youth!

If my frankness offends you, it's because I'm telling the unadulterated truth!

What is a role model in 2019? What has our community become? You have to make your back arch so stans can make you feel like you're actually someone?

Try being a leader, dare to be different!

Oh, that's scary? You were different to start with, blending in isn't in your destiny's vocabulary!

>   You have to be odd to be number one,
>   and once you get that. . .

>   Your life has truly begun!

READER'S NOTES . . .

James 4:1-2 "What causes quarrels and what causes fights among you? Is it not this, that your passions are at war within you? 2 You desire and do not have, so you murder. You covet and cannot obtain, so you fight and quarrel. You do not have, because you do not ask."

DON'T FIGHT THE SIDE CHICK

James 4:1-2

Why do you have beef with her? Was she also YOUR girl?

Why can he sit back and relax, while you do things that will make you catch a case? Can you even see the stupid look on HIS face?

Why does the man always get off the hook?? Why does the other female have you so SHOOK?

He doesn't want either of you, but of course here you are playing the fool. Ranting and raving, over some overrated tool!

You can do better, Sis! Deal with HIM instead of making all these females part of your hit list!

Find some dignity, own some pride...

Get enough courage to tell that loser: "Boy, bye!"

It's okay to move on, it's okay to remove yourself from the lies! Even you know that you're wasting your own time.

He comes home to you every night, because the side chick is smart enough to not let him live off her!

Now, leave him alone. . .

>	Become "Every Woman" so you'll attract a
>	love that you deserve.

READER'S NOTES . . .

Romans 14:19 "So then let us pursue what makes for peace and for mutual upbuilding."

BLACK LIVES MATTER?

Romans 14:19

When will black lives matter to . . . BLACK people?

How come every other race can unite and level up, but we just can't catch a break? It's because we refuse to; downright don't want to!

In my personal opinion, when we say "Black Lives Matter," we really mean our safety, our existing.

But we could not care less about our living. Since when do we support each other's LIVING?

We don't support each other's businesses, and if someone supports our business, we feel like we don't have to give them good customer service.

It seems like we always find a way to try to sabotage each other. Whether it be financially, physically, spiritually, or mentally.

This is definitely why we can't have nice things. Because we love to tear each other down. And the sad part is, "They" laugh at us.

Yes. "Them." The ones who aid in pitting us against each other. You know exactly who I'm speaking of so I don't have to go any further.

I'm sure if the supremacists and the tea party could ask us any question it would be: "Don't you realize you're black, too?"

Why? Because we play into #teamlightskinned and #teamdarkskinned.

And every other system created to divide us. The only remedy to all of these shenanigans is for us to finally UNITE and become ONE!

Stop killing. Stop beating. Stop mistreating each other!

Start supporting. Start celebrating. Start collaborating. Start praying for each other.

"Their" biggest phobia is to see us united.

>But once we do so, we will stop dying.

READER'S NOTES . . .

Romans 8:28 "And we know that for those who love God all things work together for good, for those who are called according to his purpose."

LIVE YOUR BEST LIFE

Romans 8:28

Living your best life doesn't always mean enjoying the most expensive tea and crumpets while being on a private jet to Norway!

It doesn't mean you're wealthy and have it all together.

It doesn't always mean you're an Instagram baddie, doing false advertisements for money!

It doesn't mean you met Prince Charming and he does all the things you like.

Now please don't get me wrong: if you want those things or have those things, there's nothing wrong with that.

Just hear me out for a second...

Living your best life is a state of mind! A lot of celebrities have it "all" but still don't have it all because they have no joy!

Living your best life is YOUR responsibility!

Every day, wake up and decide to be happy and make the best out of each day!

Learning to be thankful over the "small things," while not sweating the small stuff:

>...That's living your best life!

READER'S NOTES . . .

Proverbs 7:4 "Say to wisdom, "You are my sister, and call insight your intimate friend."

ALLOW INSPIRATION

Proverbs 7:4

Why can't we as women celebrate each other?

Why is there so much jealousy? Wait, I guess that's just a people problem in general. Guys do this too.

Here's what I think: when you are inspired by someone, do not gossip about them and don't try to tear them down. Don't dig up their dirt.

How about you ask them for advice? And surround yourself with their greatness? People love to talk about themselves, and it's a very high chance they will be more than happy to share their creative process or work ethic system with you!

Learn from them. However, you don't have to become them.

Take everything they have given you and apply their wisdom to your own life and you'll be on your way.

We all get 24 hours; some people just use their time better than others.

> At the end of the day I'm just saying we can all learn from each other!

READER'S NOTES . . .

Philippians 4:8 "Finally, brothers, whatever is true, whatever is honorable, whatever is just, whatever is pure, whatever is lovely, whatever is commendable, if there is any excellence, if there is anything worthy of praise, think about these things."

TEENAGE GIRL

Philippians 4:8

Let's see. I texted him at 8:30am.

It's now 11:55pm.

I thought we had a good time yesterday.

I just knew he, of all people, wouldn't be the one to play.

Maybe I should text him again? Yeah, just one more text. That may do the trick.

But am I willing to lose my pride? Oh, wow!

He just liked another girl's pictures; all of them! Yes, I counted. I'm about to start pouting!

WHAT?

He just wrote a status?

But he ain't got time to like my selfie??

Well, let me check my Snapchat archives for bomb selfies! I will show him!

Yep. I like this one, I'm about to tap post! Still nothing!

Why is he going ghost? Did I laugh too much? Did I say the wrong thing?

Was it the way I ate? Either way, he shouldn't make me wait!

Maybe a breakup is necessary. I have a lot on my plate!

You know what? I saw the signs that he had something wrong with him and still I took the bait!

Oh never mind. Silly me.

I forgot to press "Send."

                He wasn't really ignoring me!

READER'S NOTES . . .

Revelation 21:4 "He will wipe away every tear from their eyes, and death shall be no more, neither shall there be mourning, nor crying, nor pain anymore, for the former things have passed away."

GRIEF

Revelation 21:4

Like an eagle with wings, you had to soar.

I am overcome with emotions to match my tribulations.

Here I am picking up the pieces, because you aren't here anymore.

Now the tears run down my face, because in my mind I constantly see yours.

This type of feeling cannot be ignored. One thing I know for sure is grief is absolutely unequivocal proof that you've loved someone.

Whether it is a friend, or a relative, or even if it's two hearts that became one.

Like a camel in the desert longing for just a drop of water is how I long to hear your voice one more time. I wish you could give me one small thing to cling to.

Because in reality you never think that the last time you see a healthy person is indeed the LAST time! Fast and quick you went. Painfully and dreadfully.

I must move on. I know inside that's what you would've wanted for me all along. You'd tell me to be strong.

Golden Tones: Writing With Soul

You are now where you truly belong; walking along streets of gold and hearing the best choir songs.

Comforted by the fact that your blood still pumps in my veins;

    I can rest in the fact that you're no longer in pain.

READER'S NOTES . . .

Matthew 11:28-30 "Come to me, all who labor and are heavy laden, and I will give you rest. 29 Take my yoke upon you, and learn from me, for I am gentle and lowly in heart, and you will find rest for your souls. 30 For my yoke is easy, and my burden is light."

CHURCH HURT

Matthew 11:28-30

I don't wear the latest lace front, nor don the perfect outfit. But what I do have is a genuine heart and a story.

I see the way you laugh at me when I walk into the sanctuary, with my child born out of wedlock. My baby will always look good, even if I have to look halfway decent.

This is the second time I've tried coming to church on a weekly basis. The first time I left, I was abused by the deacon.

When I was denied the chance to sing on the praise team for being pregnant, I felt like I had nothing.

That I was worth.... nothing.

I used to be the "golden child that had to walk more than half a mile" just to come to church on Sunday.

I wasn't rich as ya'll; that alone set me apart from your 'boujee' way of living. I saw the way you all treated the other abused people in the church. And if I'm honest, I participated in the shenanigans just to fit in.

I too acted like a jerk. I did it for the simple fact that I thought it could never happen to me, but if it did you guys would have my back.

Or so I thought until I turned seventeen. These things happen more often than our community will ever come clean about. Then when my Great Uncle preaches you have the nerve to shout?

Knowing all the people's needs and how tragedy is just swept under the rug, like it never happened. It will be a wonder if half of ya'll even make it to heaven.

Even after all of this I still refuse to leave again. The things that happened removed my heart from my sleeve. I will just focus on making God my everything; I'm staying faithful to Him alone and waiting on all He has for me. When the time is right, every wrong will be made right concerning me.

I just wish there would be one person in this tabernacle who would take time to learn me . . .

> . . . instead of attempting to break me.

READER'S NOTES . . .

Colossians 3:12-14 "Put on then, as God's chosen ones, holy and beloved, compassionate hearts, kindness, humility, meekness, and patience, 13 bearing with one another and, if one has a complaint against another, forgiving each other; as the Lord has forgiven you, so you also must forgive. 14 And above all these put on love, which binds everything together in perfect harmony."

REAL LOVE

Colossians 3:12-14

As I began to focus on myself, and be all about "Me" again, I can honestly say that I was taking a break from men.

Every day I took myself on dates. I learned to walk in my purpose and to love myself.

And then I knew finally that I was "Worth It!"

I was worth everything that I prayed for and I became thankful for every closed door I had encountered.

Then suddenly. . .

You came.

You took charge and made your intentions and vision concerning being in my life extremely plain. When my friends and family would see me smile, they would forget that I was ever in pain.

You were consistent, you were true and honest. We met in June, and you started courting me the first week in August; the eighth month.

I find no irony here, because you are evidence that new beginnings do exist. Thank you for always putting me first on your list, after God and yourself, of course.

You constantly remind me that I belong to Jesus And I rejoice in that, in return for the nice things you do for me, you never required me to give up my body.

For this, I know that God himself can trust us. I thoroughly enjoy our church and dinner dates. When it comes to taking me out, you have never been late.

This is our last day being engaged. And tomorrow before God, and hundreds, I will start my vows with: "For this man have I prayed."

This man that I have fallen for.

This man who has brought me closer to the Lord. This man who has supported my calling.

Thank you for confirming to me what true love is.

> The kind of love that you can't
> receive from any Wiz.

READER'S NOTES . . .

Psalm 90:17 "Let the favor of the Lord our God be upon us and establish the work of our hands upon us, yes, establish the work of our hands."

GRANDMA'S HANDS: FOR OMEALIA

Psalm 90: 17

G randma's hands had long nails on each finger.
With no room to linger, a ring on each finger.

Grandma's hands made the best ramen noodles and crab legs.

Grandma's hands attempted to teach me to crochet.

Grandma's hands taught me how to curl hair.

Grandma's hands grabbed corrections rods when needed.

Grandma's hands took many, many pictures.

Grandma's hands made gorgeous knitted dresses for baby dolls.

Grandma's hands drove me to vacation Bible school.

Grandma's hands taught me how to use a remote.

Grandma's hands use to hit me after she cracked a joke.

Grandma's hands were the hands that never broke.

Grandma's hands are now intertwined with the Lord's.

READER'S NOTES . . .

John 16:21 "When a woman is giving birth, she has sorrow because her hour has come, but when she has delivered the baby, she no longer remembers the anguish, for joy that a human being has been born into the world."

MAMA'S HEART

John 16:21

Mama's heart is the most difficult to interpret. She gives and gives and gives until she becomes empty.

She is the most misunderstood in the family. She sees things that no one else could possibly see.

Often pushed away for auntie and grandma; loving her child wholeheartedly is one thing she is not afraid of.

Mama doesn't mind pretending to be the enemy; it hurts her but as long as her child is happy!

She lets her teenager say whatever she says in order to make herself feel better.

Mama's love - in spite of - will not change.

She is well aware that at times she can never "Get it right."

But still sees the relationship with her young as being worth the fight.

She takes care of her rebellious, angry child always, even during her own sick nights.

Mama's love can hold us too tight at times.

But we only have one of her.

    Let's make a conscious decision to treat her right.

READER'S NOTES . . .

Proverbs 23:29-30 "Who has woe? Who has sorrow? Who has strife? Who has complaining?

Who has wounds without cause? Who has redness of eyes? 30 Those who tarry long over wine; those who go to try mixed wine."

JUST ONE MORE DRINK

Proverbs 23:29-30

One drink won't hurt, right?

I've had a rough day. My boss acted a plum fool.

He was obnoxious and rude every time he came my way.

That drink was delicious, but it didn't calm my nerves.

I think I need just one more. Just one more drink, only so I don't have to think about my predicament.

That second drink was okay, but I'm still on edge. I'm drinking my third drink.

Now we are talking. Heck, I even forget where I'm currently working.

What's my Boss's name? Ronnie? Bill? Hmm. It will come back to me.

I feel so tempted looking at my car keys.

0.8 is all I need to hurt myself, or someone else.

And I could easily become that loser who could not avoid drinking and driving on the news.

Is it worth it? NOPE!

Excuse me, Mr. Bartender sir, call me an Uber! The last thing I want is to become a DUI loser.

Take my keys. I will be back in the morning. Stressed or not, I still try to live responsibly.

    My family and other families in society will thank me.

READER'S NOTES . . .

***Ecclesiastes 5:3** "For a dream comes with much business, and a fool's voice with many words."*

BETTER

Ecclesiastes 5:3

There's nothing wrong with dreaming of better.

Do YOU ever dream of better?

I'm not talking about the times where Michigan's weather goes from winter to spring. I'm talking about that feeling when we decide to be a go- getter and chase after our own dreams.

Not the dreams mama or daddy, best friend, or the family have for you.

Your own dreams.

I can't speak for you personally, but as for me.

I wanna be where the people are.

I wanna be with the shooting stars.

I wanna be where no one can touch me, where the wind is beneath my feet.

In that special place where no one can take away my dreams.

Let's do it today! Let's go after the thing that keeps us awake.

That's the only way we will take the stage, the successful stage of life.

Success is so close, so close to being mine.

> My biggest fear is not wanting better for myself,
> and being left behind.

READER'S NOTES . . .

Psalm 37:1-2 "Fret not yourself because of evildoers; be not envious of wrongdoers!

2 For they will soon fade like the grass and wither like the green herb."

BLUE SKIES

Psalm 37:1-2

Don't you dare tamper with my blue skies!
You can never take them away from me.

Don't be mad at me because you are too blind to see your own. You literally detest seeing the beauty in life!

Don't be jaded because you refuse to walk through your own open doors.

Doors which only you could walk through. I'm high stepping through mine.

I celebrate my small beginnings.

That way when I finally "make it," my accomplishments will have a more profound feeling.

Why huff and puff when you see me, when you could be doing your own thing with meaning?

I'm not cocky about my life path, I'm just inspired.

I'm just open-minded.

You don't have to detest people for making plans and following through; expand your own horizons. When you give your own destiny a chance...

That's when you too can join the dance.

READER'S NOTES . . .

Proverbs 3:31 "Do not envy a man of violence and do not choose any of his ways. . . ."

IT WAS A ONE TIME THING

Proverbs 3:31

It was a one-time thing.

Unpunished and unchecked.

It led to everything.

We got into an argument one night. He called me out my name. I let it go because I thought it was a one-time thing.

A few weeks after that, he shoved me into the wall because his food was cold in the middle while his plate burned his hand. I let it go because I thought it was a one-time thing. He sent roses to my job and I told my boss that he felt bad that I ran into the door. That whole week, my entire upper body was extra sore.

A few months went by and nothing gruesome happened, leading me to believe that he changed his stripes. After all it was only a one-time thing.

Next thing I knew, he gave me a black eye on Thanksgiving and a deliberate burn from the iron. I put some concealer on and made sure I wore long sleeves. I went to go eat dinner with him and my in laws because I thought it was a one-time thing.

Last week, I finally tried to leave. He cried so manipulatively and told me I was his everything. I stayed in spite of the warning from relatives, friends, my boss, my pastor, and even my enemies.

He eventually started hitting me in public. He made disruptive scenes. Not caring about being arrested, or even my own humiliation.

But today we got into a heated argument over me wanting to spend Christmas with my grandmother and the kids without him.

He said he knew about the other man; a man who didn't even exist.

He ended my life once and for all.

I ignored the red flags from the start because I never thought the one who I loved, he one who gave my heart butterflies could also. . .

Make my heart stop.

READER'S NOTES . . .

John 3:16 "For God so loved the world, that he gave his only Son, that whoever believes in him should not perish but have eternal life."

JESUS

John 3:16

He loves me at my worst moments, when no one else is there.

He holds me close when all I can do is cry and no one else seems to care.

He takes me by my hand, holding it firm like any good Father would.

He leads me down a brighter path each and every day.

When the nights are long and my mind feels gone, He's the lamp that I need for my soul to calm.

He's the one who proves me wrong when I feel like I can't succeed.

More than that, before I was even born, He bowed His head and died for me. He died so I can live for Him with a beautiful song to sing.

I always need Him to stay close to me; I'm living in a dying world.

When I'm not feeling so sure about life. . .

> He lets me know that I'm His girl!

READER'S NOTES . . .

Proverbs 27:17 "Iron sharpens iron, and one man sharpens another."

GOOD VIBEZ ONLY

Proverbs 27:17

At almost 21, I can say I'm starting to feel a little bit different.

I just want to be happy. I'll get rid of anyone who drains my spirit.

The ones who always try to belittle me, the ones who refuse to feel me.

I want to make the best of my twenties.

I hate pointless small talk, but we can have a wholesome, enlightening conversation for hours.

I want people around me who challenge me to be better; people who are a little wiser!

The kind of people that can take me higher. And vice versa!

If it costs me my peace of mind and my happiness, I just simply cannot afford it!

I'm trying to grow to become the best me. Not so I can be seen, but so that life and love flow from within me.

I want to have a positive outlook, even when I'm not on Facebook.

I would rather be alone than to be surrounded by bad company.

    Especially the ones who are not for me.

READER'S NOTES . . .

Proverbs 27:6 "Faithful are the wounds of a friend; profuse are the kisses of an enemy."

A FRIEND

Proverbs 27:6

What constitutes a good friend in the current century? Well, definitions may vary.

At times the definition of a true friend is mistaken for an enemy.

People love to think that if a person isn't your "Yes" man, then they are not a real friend. But do they ever stop to think that the "No" wasn't intended to offend?

A true friend will be honest with you whether you like it or not. Even if you threaten to cut them off. Because they are too real and authentic to allow you to go out in the real world and look pathetic.

Not everyone is your hater; some people *want* to see you succeed. Quit pushing people with sound doctrine away and learn how to take heed!

Listen to understand instead of partially hearing and then responding.

Your friends try to warn you because they did what you currently want to do and their life went wrong. Nowhere in the Bible does it say: "Love agrees with everything you do."

Your true friends love you. That's why they try to tell you that there is a better way!

Not everyone has venom inside of them.

>   Hear them out and see what they are trying to say!

READER'S NOTES . . .

1 Corinthians 10:13 "There hath no temptation taken you but such as is common to man: but God is faithful, who will not suffer you to be tempted above that ye are able; but will with the temptation also make a way to escape, that ye may be able to bear it." (KJV)

ROUGH AND TOUGH ADDICTIONS

1 Corinthians 10:13

Why did I try it? Because I thought that one time wouldn't make or break my life. I had no idea about the strife, the tension, or the heartbreak my action that day would cause.

I still do it because every day I chase the first time feeling; that released dopamine feeling. I need to feel the chills in my spine.

Just one more time.

I never thought I could ever let it get this bad, or that I would ever go this far. I know I should've said no from the start.

I knew it was wrong to put the needle to my arm, the bottle to my mouth. Seems like once I tried them both, my life went down south.

I stopped caring about the things that were important to me. The alcohol and the drugs have me so blind to the treasures that life holds that I can no longer see.

I tell my kids, my siblings, and nephews, "Do as I say, and not as I do!" whenever I'm questioned about why they aren't allowed to use my stuff.

I used to be the example. I was the person everyone looked up to. Now look at me, I'm stealing my mom's minks, my brothers' watches, and my grandmothers' purses.

   All for these faulty dime bags.

And to make things worse, I can hear the cries and the prayers from my mother's room. One time I even heard her say "Donna, I never thought it would ever be you."

This addiction made me grow up too fast. I hated my youth.

I wanted to fit in and now I'm in deep.

   Buried inside of my addictions.

It was on my own free will, I refuse to call it an affliction. This isn't a game, it's surely not fiction. Say "No!" like I should've. That will be your very best action.

Remind your peers of how dangerous this can be.

   You might cause a chain reaction.

READER'S NOTES . . .

Psalm 27:10 "For my father and my mother have forsaken me, but the Lord will take me in."

REJECTION

Psalm 27:10

As my heart broke, your heart turned cold. As I reached out to you consistently, you constantly shut me down. What did I do wrong this time?

Yes. I said this time because you always play these games.

We are all adults here; because of the way you act sometimes you should really be ashamed.

I've done all that I can but you always have to show you still have the upper hand.

You go out of your way to show me that I'm unwelcome in your life.

But it's alright. I'm moving on now, so I will get over these feelings of strife.

Had you been a friend, I'd be upset, but after time, okay with it.

But since you're family, it's harder for my heart to bear it.

However, once I heal, don't try to deal with me again.

I took the hint; you had me bent.

> I'm not sad, just annoyed about all the
> wasted time we spent.

READER'S NOTES . . .

Mark 10:14 "But when Jesus saw it, he was indignant and said to them, "Let the children come to me; do not hinder them, for to such belongs the kingdom of God."

I GOT SOME CANDY!

Mark 10:14

I got some candy!

After you told me to stop all that crying.

You warned me, STERNLY warned me, not to tell nobody. Because if I did you'd say: "She's lying!"

I didn't think anything of it, when I would fall asleep in my toddler bed and wake up to find you sitting on the edge.

I didn't think anything of it when I would go to the bathroom, open the door when I got finished, see you standing outside the door as if you were waiting for me the whole time.

I was so stupid, how did I not see it coming? I was clearly being sized up and didn't know it! That's what I've been telling myself for years now.

I wasn't afraid of anything. I had no phobias of nothing.

Until this happened.

Until you did what you did. It's hard for me to see you, knowing my parents don't know.

It's awkward for me to see you act like you caught the "Holy Ghost" on Sunday. It's even more disheartening when my parents force me to speak to you, or (even worse) make me hug you because they don't know the truth.

They've never met the REAL you.

All of my older girl cousins refuse to come around you. Did you hurt them as well?

Did they get candy too?

READER'S NOTES . . .

1 Corinthians 13:4-5 4. "Love is patient and kind; love does not envy or boast; it is not arrogant or rude. 5. It does not insist on its own way; it is not irritable or resentful."

NO REAL COMMITMENT

1 Corinthians 13:4-5

You have been my full time lover with part time feelings.

Your looks are so intriguing.

Endearing words spill out of your pillow soft lips that you know I love to hear. Each sentence you form is the cause of you being the one that I adore.

I ignorantly gave you everything: my soul, my body. And something I can't take back: my time. Why do I stay here?

Because in the beginning you were the one who made me feel comfortable when I really needed to unwind.

Because you hypnotize me with your kisses, the sense of hope that I will become your "Mrs." gets smaller and smaller.

I fear that at any time, you will get tired of me and abruptly throw me away.

I fear that you will give another woman what I've waited over a decade for.

She would never put up with you like I did. I've truly been your ride or die. I went through hell and back for you. Gave up all I was just to be able to brag that I had you by my side.

If my biggest fear does indeed happen, I know that nothing I did for the love of you will even make a difference to you.

Because there was no real commitment.

READER'S NOTES . . .

Psalm 139:16 "Your eyes saw my unformed substance; in your book were written, every one of them, the days that were formed for me, when as yet there was none of them."

ONE DAY CHILD

Psalm 139:16

A lot of people take having children lightly. That's a scary thing to fathom. I don't have all of the answers concerning the correct way to raise a child, but I feel that it's never too early to take

them into consideration before they arrive. If I could say anything to my future child it would be

along the lines of . . .

I don't know you.

You don't know me. We haven't met yet. But still you keep me going.

Although you're not currently in my life yet, it feels like you are very much a part of me.

I can't just give up on my dreams like that. You're my legacy.

Every day, I try to walk in faith, and go after the things that I can't yet see.

I have to make wise choices now so you don't suffer later. How is it that you're technically the perfect stranger, yet can still have such a huge impact on my life?

I will let you know from jump-street that I won't be perfect.

I will make mistakes. It's fair, I guess because you will make a few too.

But just know that your shortcomings will never take away or change. . .

    The love I already have for you.

READER'S NOTES . . .

Daniel 1:17 "As for these four youths, God gave them learning and skill in all literature and wisdom, and Daniel had understanding in all visions and dreams."

SCHOOL EDUCATED ME

Daniel 1:17

"School ain't for everybody."

People enjoy saying that, don't they? I once believed that. However, I did learn some stuff about life along the way.

Plenty of times, while being in school, I learned how to go hard for myself! If I don't have my own back, and actually show that, I won't be able to depend on anyone else to have it!

I learned that there will be times where you do the most work, and the slackers will get the same score as you. That can definitely cause an attitude.

I learned on the other hand that if one person slacks, the whole group could also get a bad grade! How's that for some rain on your parade?

I learned that it's important to meet people. You never know who you could really be sitting next to.

I learned that time is of great essence.

You can't get it back.

However, time is the one thing that is often played with. And then – finally - I learned that it's okay to ask questions.

The humility it takes to ask something in front of the whole class is truly a blessing.

That is because The "Know-It-All's" usually don't know it all.

So if you want to go to school, don't allow anyone to make you feel like a "Fool."

> You have great resilience that will be
> reflected in your brilliance!

READER'S NOTES . . .

Matthew 5:14 "You are the light of the world. A city set on a hill cannot be hidden."

BE THAT ONE LIGHT

Matthew 5:14

We live in a society that is all about "Me, me, me."

We are often too preoccupied with our own selfishness to see the needs of others: children without mothers, mothers without daughters and people without money.

I say this to encourage you.

If you see someone with a need, be that light. Instead of whipping your iPhone out and recording the scene, break up that fight.

When the elderly lady is struggling with a ton of groceries, how much would it cost you to help her? Because one day you just may be her!

When that young man has the world on his shoulders and a sad look on his face, it won't take any skin off your nose to show some grace.

If society would just keep this in mind, we would be so much better off.

Give love, receive love. Make someone's day.

Love on each other; learn how to become one.

> We can do this daily until there's nothing left to do under the sun.

READER'S NOTES . . .

Exodus 23:1 "You shall not spread a false report. You shall not join hands with a wicked man to be a malicious witness."

GOSSIP BUG

Exodus 23:1

If the gossip bug bites you, make sure you also tell the good things about me.

Tell your little friends that I can sing.

Tell your nosy friends that I can act.

Not that I would ever expect you to have my back.

Get my story right: don't talk about me half way. Just sayin'.

If the gossip bug bites you concerning me, it means I'm on your mind.

That's beneficial to me, because it's still press!

However, I can't exactly say what it is for you.

And, by the way, would it hurt to add in a few truths?

And finally, when your little chit-chat is done, don't try to cover your 'ratchedness' by running up to me with your fake . . .

"He said, she said" mess!

READER'S NOTES . . .

***John 15:13** "Greater love has no one than this, that someone lay down his life for his friends."*

"SOUL SISTAH"

John 15:13

You're my ride or die; my girl from way back. The one that I can always go to when I got the munchies and need a snack! Girl, you always have my back.

You keep my secrets, you tell me no lies. You even teach me how to talk to the guys!

You are wise beyond your years; you've helped me conquer many of my fears!

I'm so glad you've been in my company for all these ten long years!

What I do for you in return is nothing to sneeze at! I tell you when you have lipstick on your teeth, and when your clothes don't match!

I'm the fashionista; you're the one with brains. We are so different from each other. But in many ways, we are one in the same.

Uh huh, yeah; we both 'home girls" from Detroit. We love to make lots of noise and we know the joy of growing up on Livernois.

I hope we can be friends and sistahs for life, letting no circumstances or any man come in between us.

Let's fight for what we have with all of our might! Let's promise to listen to each other and never judge or back bite.

And when things go south...

> Let's communicate until we can make things right!

READER'S NOTES . . .

Romans 12:2 "Do not be conformed to this world,[a] but be transformed by the renewal of your mind, that by testing you may discern what is the will of God, what is good and acceptable and perfect."[b]

TEAM NATURAL

Romans 12:2

A lot of people swear that I'm made up of that "rough and tough stuff."

That may be true, but what is it to YOU?

Why do the naps and curls and swirls that grow from my head make you see red?

I'm sorry but I can't sit in a chair for eight hours to get braids only to end up with no edges.

I refuse to get a kiddie perm, and no it's not just because it will burn.

And the hot comb? Forget it, because I'm not down with it!

The flat iron and blow dryer is only a "Once in a While Thing."

I just don't see why being natural isn't always trendy; why "going natural" has become such a big thing?

Weren't we born like this?

If you ask me (which you probably won't), there's no need to assimilate into what I'm not when I can just appreciate what I am.

Just sayin' . . .

Golden Tones: Writing With Soul

READER'S NOTES . . .

Proverbs 14:15 "The simple believes everything, but the prudent gives thought to his steps."

BY THE LOCKERS

Proverbs 14:15

Every day.

I wake up real early.

No, seriously, really, *really* early.

Just so I can pick out the right outfit. And make sure my hair is on point.

What for? I'm glad you asked. There's this tall, handsome, dark and smooth boy in my class. His name is Samuel.

Everyone just calls him Sam. His locker is right next to mine. He has never had a girlfriend before!

My heart races every time he walks through that one door. He is so fine. . .

        I clearly just want him to be mine.

In class, he smiles at me then looks away; I think he's shy.

I wait for him by the lockers, so I can have a close up look at his face. Maybe if he sees how good I look, it will have him shook.

He will be mine in no time! But back to his face; there's no wrinkles, no pimples, and not a hair out of place.

If he catches me staring at him, will he bring out the mace? WAIT!

Look there he is!

"Hey, Sam! Quick question for ya! Will you be my boyfriend?"

No? Uhm, okay, thanks. Sorry about my outburst! Enjoy your next class!"

OMG! For our first conversation ever, I think that went pretty well!

He is so totally into me! Like straight up obsessed with me! Fo' real he is.

                    Can't you tell?

READER'S NOTES . . .

Proverbs 4:1-2 "Hear, O sons, a father's instruction, and be attentive, that you may gain insight. 2. for I give you good precepts; do not forsake my teaching."

LATE

Proverbs 4:1-2

I thought that I was invincible. As if the consequences that I've seen on other girls' face didn't apply to me.

Even though I was doing the same exact thing.

No lecture from mama, no required class at school, or the warnings from my sisters, cool aunties, and cousins were taken heed to.

I was dismissive of them all. Pride comes before the fall. Warning comes before destruction, and a hard head makes a soft behind.

That's the only language I could understand at the time. But he was so "cool." Absolutely "sexy." And way too popular to pass up!

I let him get too close to me when I should have kept him at the same distance as my enemy. He only saw me for the moment, but even in that I was too blind to see. I swore up and down that I was his only woman.

But now look at me, alone, embarrassed, and worst of all fearful. I can barely afford McDonald's!

How can I get this kid through college? What kind of help can I offer this unborn child of mine?

I better speak up now; there's such a short and limited time that I can hide!

Hide from my family, and my stomach.

If I could talk to any other girl, or the girl I was a month ago, I would tell her that it's just not worth it!

Keep your head in the books.

>   Please keep your eyes off that boy
>   with the good looks.

READER'S NOTES . . .

Psalm 34:17-19 "When the righteous cry for help, the Lord hears and delivers them out of all their troubles. 18 The Lord is near to the brokenhearted and saves the crushed in spirit. 19 Many are the afflictions of the righteous, but the Lord delivers him out of them all."

IF YOU GAVE UP TODAY

Psalm 34:17-19

If you gave up today, there would be a huge price to pay.

The ones who would be the most in anguish would be your family.

They would have the kind of pain that the natural eye cannot see. Quit saying you want to die.

Because it's not true.

Hold on for just a while longer so I can explain this to you. If you weren't experiencing this pain you feel, you'd want to be here still!

You would be down to chill. You wouldn't want to risk losing the many joys and simple things in life; things such as finding more fries at the bottom of the bag or feeling a nice cool breeze once you exit a hot building.

You'd miss that eleventh chicken nugget in your ten-piece piece meal. Or the new hit song of the upcoming year. These are the things you enjoy right now; these are the times that you hold dear!

Ever stop to think that maybe you're someone's pleasure in life? Think that having you - yes, I said **you** - around can put an end to their frown?

I'm not one to judge, but it would be pretty selfish to let them down! Please hear me out, You are a priceless, limited edition. You're unique, there's no one else on this planet that's exactly like YOU!

It's safe to say that you are very much needed! You too make the world go round! Someone needs you here so that they can make it! I know that you will make it! Everyday you open your eyes is a brand new chance at life!

So for all of the amazing things you'd miss out on, and the people that love you and need you: I challenge you to take it! Seize that opportunity to be happy and to heal!

> You'll be glad you did, and that's the real deal!

Chelsea G. Robinson

READER'S NOTES . . .

Philippians 4:13 "I can do all things through him who strengthens me."

FEAR

Philippians 4:13

New chapters in my life are unfolding and I'm not sure how to handle it all.

Will I make it with flying colors, like I intend to? Or will I just stumble and fall? Will I fall too hard? If I do, will I be able to get back up, back up in one piece?

Will I have the ability to put my broken pieces back together? I'm nervous; self-doubt is no joke. Will I rise proudly to this new opportunity, or will I choke?

Fear of the unknown is trying to pull me back. But on the other hand, this is all I have ever wanted! A degree, with my own name on it!

I went and got my associate's degree just so I could see that the girl I see every day in the mirror, that smart girl, was indeed me.

Will I make a difference? Is there anything about me, anything at all. . .

That is inspirational?

What qualities do I possess inside that can help me stand tall?

Mama always told me, while I was coming up, that I could do anything that I put my mind to. But each time I reach new successes and new heights, I tend to think that this is the end. "This is the best you can possibly do," I tend to think to myself.

Am I making a foolish mistake by going back to school, even though I said I would never do that again? Or will it be smooth sailing, a harmonic experience or will I be worried about irrational things?

I don't know for sure, but somewhere I read that I can do all things through God Who strengthens me.

So I guess you could say the only one who can actually stop me . . .

Is me.

READER'S NOTES . . .

Jeremiah 1:5 "Before I formed you in the womb I knew you, and before you were born I consecrated you; I appointed you a prophet to the nations."

ABORTION

Jeremiah 1:5

"My mama is gonna kill me," 15-year old Teena though as she exited the doors of the free clinic.

And you know what, if Teena's sweet, sweet baby, who was only six weeks along could speak, she'd say the same thing.

Tears rolled down Teena's face.

"How could I be so irresponsible? Why didn't I just go to the movies with Aleesha that night, like I told Mama that I was going to?"

"How will I make it being only 15. A single mother?"

She thought these deep, frightening thoughts because Derrick was nowhere to be found.

Yeah, they would see one another at school but often times he treated her like a ghost. And she was definitely not his only boo.

The bus ride home was the longest, coldest, scariest time Teena had ever experienced.

"Maybe I can get rid of it" she thought. "I can just erase my mistakes, and make this all go away. Especially before everything goes too far and I am exposed."

She finally made it home, got off the bus, and thought she was home alone. She made a quick call to the abortion clinic, made an appointment, and hung up the phone.

"Hi sugar, are you busy tonight?" Grandmother said, as she came from the kitchen. "I made your favorite, chicken gumbo, with extra rice."

She spoke softly as she slowly limped in Teena's direction, to show her some affection.

When Grandmother touched her, Teena's heart dropped in her stomach and she began to weep bitter tears.

"Grandma, I can't eat," she wailed. "Do you still love me?" she cried.

Grandmother held Teena tightly. "Let's sit down."

Teena poured her heart out to her Grandmother.

"Oh, Grandma, I'm so hurt," Teena moaned. "I'm unlovable. I'm worthless. I'm a mistake."

Teena sat with her head bowed low.

"I made an appointment to fix everything that I've done, before mama and the school finds out."

Grandmother gave her girl a compassionate smile and placed her warm, wrinkled hand on top of Teena's.

"Girlfriend, you are none of those horrible things you've labeled yourself," Grandma whispered in her papery soft voice. "But I guarantee that the way you see yourself right now will be all of the thoughts that will go through your sweet baby's head, while pain is being inflicted on it. Pain inflicted for a crime it personally did not commit."

Teena's eyes widened in shock.

"Grandma, what do you mean by that?"

Grandma sighed: "Your child will also feel unloved, worthless, like they are a mistake during the abortion process." Grandma said frankly. "If you don't want to feel that way, don't make anyone else feel like that either. Just think about it."

Grandma stood up slowly and started to walk away before turning back to Teena.

"By the way, your mama made the decision to keep her baby 15 years ago".

Grandma smirked, as she left the room to leave Teena to register everything she heard.

"Maybe I can still graduate. Maybe things won't be as bad as I anticipate. If mama can be successful I can too."

Teena reached for her iPhone, "Hello, I'd like to cancel my appointment. I've changed my mind. No ma'am, nothing is wrong."

> "I just believe that for once, I will be just fine."

READER'S NOTES . . .

Micah 6:8 "He has told you, O man, what is good; and what does the Lord require of you

but to do justice, and to love kindness, and to walk humbly with your God?"

BEFORE U APPROACH ME

Micah 6:8

I know I am cute.

Yeah, I get it. "I'm 'fine'."

But that doesn't give you an open invitation to waste my time.

How dare you awaken my love with no intentions to maintain something legit?

How dare you try to fill my mind with empty hopes and dreams! Have me longing for the real thing. You lead me on; have me all excited for **what**? Nothing you have presented to me in reality is worth writing home about.

And then when I start to doubt you, you make it seem like I am the problem.

My real problem is that I and my sisters are tired; tired of the games, the foolishness, and the lies. What do you gain from acting goofy?

But you sit in judgment of us and claim that we girls are "moody?"

Seriously?

You don't even know what you want hour-by-hour. And if a real man shows interest in me, you get upset and care now? Nope, keep your same lack of energy.

Keep doing what you've been doing. Before you approach me, have your stuff together. Come correct. Lose the other girls. And make sure you have a job that gives you a check!

Don't talk a fake game then pull away if I say the feeling is mutual. I want you too. Don't use fear as your excuse, and don't treat me like an option.

Before you drop the ball with a woman, remember she can be your biggest blessing or your hardest lesson. And don't forget this . . .

> It's really up to you.

Chelsea G. Robinson

READER'S NOTES . . .

Psalm 102:24 "O my God," I say, "Take me not away in the midst of my days, you whose years endure throughout all generations!"

TO PAC . . .

Psalm 102:24

Whenever I look at your photo, I'm overwhelmed.

You were a beautiful human being. But that's not all there was to you. You had intelligence. You weren't afraid to use your mind, to think for yourself. And you challenged those around you, and those who allowed themselves to be reached by you, to do the same.

You weren't one to think inside the box, that is what so many loved about you. You had an indescribable charm about yourself. You could woo any woman with your smile. With many accomplishments under your belt by the tender age of 25, I hope you found life worth your while.

The things you spoke of back then are still relevant in this present day. I often think "Pac called it."

Your revelatory wisdom is timeless. It's sad that your good looks, your wisdom, your talent, and the long life you had ahead of you weren't enough to prevent your untimely fate.

But one thing about you that I highly appreciate is the fact that you often spoke for the people that didn't have a voice; the ones who didn't know that they have one. You never lost sight of where you came from, no matter how successful you became.

And that's the type of woman I strive to be every day. If by chance I acquire my own platform one day, I will keep the same energy that you had.

You had your ups and downs, but I believe in my heart that, overall, you wanted to do the right thing. The fact that we as a planet had you for a quarter of a century is definitely still music to my ears.

My only hope for you now is that now you're resting. . .

>In a place where you don't have to
>shed so many tears.

READER'S NOTES . . .

Proverbs 3:5-6 "Trust in the Lord with all your heart, and do not lean on your own understanding. 6 In all your ways acknowledge him, and he will make straight your paths."

FAILURE

Proverbs 3:5-6

Isn't it funny how the very things we fear the most often end up coming our way? A lot of us have feared failure at one time, or another. But what if I told you that failure could be the best thing to happen to you, when you had your plans all thought out?

Things not going as we originally planned can make us want to scream, maybe even shout. But what I know, without a single doubt, is that when you've hit rock bottom, you can only manage to go up from there.

We think failure is the end to all we were working so hard for. But my friend, what if it's really just a fresh start, a door to something new?

Think about it, sometimes your "Plan B" can be ten times better than your "Plan A?" And with your second attempt at accomplishing your goals, you have more wisdom, and resilience about yourself.

There was something you had to learn during that first process, which is why that process needs to be embraced.

The most successful people in life have failed a million times, but they made the conscious decision to dust themselves off.

They made a decision to call a spade a spade, learn the lesson, and get back in it to run and win the race. And that's how you should be.

So tell me: are you willing to get back in the race?

And win?

READER'S NOTES . . .

Revelation 21:4 "He will wipe away every tear from their eyes, and death shall be no more, neither shall there be mourning, nor crying, nor pain anymore, for the former things have passed away."

LOSING YOU

Revelation 21:4

"**H**ow could God just take you like that?" I thought to myself as I received the news.

"Hasn't our family been through enough?"

As the tears fell down my face, I became so unfocused that I'm surprised I didn't cause an accident.

I wept and wept and cried out to God: "How come it seems like every two years I lose another aunt or yet another uncle. When will it stop?"

Well I guess it has, because you were the last one. And I was still recovering from the last time.

My Granny's siblings were so important to me. We each had our own unique bond. You took selfies with me making me feel special because I know that wasn't an everyday thing for you. I enjoyed seeing you at family functions. Sometimes just the presence of a person can make you feel complete; you were that for me.

I remember one time I came over to visit with you and our family.

That day, you remembered details about me from my childhood, especially the fact that I was a huge Bill Cosby fan as a tot. I just felt so honored that I was on your heart to the extent that you remembered something so hugely important to me.

In essence, I understand that you lived a long and prosperous life.

You were full of joy, success and raised an amazing family.

You touched many people, leaving behind a remarkable legacy.

Having a generous portion of your blood in my veins is comforting. It's a reminder that you will never be too far away.

>It will tide me over until I see you again on
>my brighter day!

READER'S NOTES . . .

2 Timothy 1:4-5 "As I remember your tears, I long to see you, that I may be filled with joy. 5 I am reminded of your sincere faith, a faith that dwelt first in your grandmother Lois and your mother Eunice and now, I am sure, dwells in you as well."

TO FLORENE

2 Timothy 1:4-5

I never got a chance to hear your voice. I never had a seat at your table. I never tasted a meal prepared by you.

Imagine what I go through on a regular basis when people tell me how amazing you were. They tell me how much you and I are similar, but I can't see it for myself. And neither can you.

Even though you transitioned two years exactly to my due date, I still feel like I've met you before! I know it sounds crazy, but it feels like somewhere, somehow we have interacted.

How can I hold my purse exactly like you, my grandmother, the one I have never seen? How can I enjoy apples and cheese, or hate wearing thick coats, preferring to feel the breeze?

Just like you did?

I mean, I am the only grandchild of yours that you never got to hold, because you didn't get to grow old. And don't get me started on our shared looks.

Grandma, do you know how much I get told that I look just like you, and your niece "D?" It's weird, when I see your photos, I do see me. Anyway, I know I get my resilience from you.

Yes, I've heard amazing stories. That's why I wish I had the chance to get advice from you just once; especially during my teens.

You were remarkable, and raised a remarkable woman, one whom I call "Mommy."

I have some huge shoes to fill. With that being said, "Thank You" for laying down an amazing foundation for me to build from.

And just know, when I make it big one day, I won't forget where I came from.

And you're part of that.

READER'S NOTES . . .

2 Corinthians 5:18-19 "All this is from God, who through Christ reconciled us to himself and gave us the ministry of reconciliation; 19 that is, in Christ God was reconciling[a] the world to himself, not counting their trespasses against them, and entrusting to us the message of reconciliation."

RECONCILIATION

2 Corinthians 5:18-19

We live in a day where cutting people out of our lives is highly celebrated.

I think as a result of this, it has become very hard to maintain relationships with our brothers and sisters and significant others.

Don't get me wrong, sometimes family can be really toxic. But I had to learn the rough way that cutting people off over misunderstandings or arguing via text messaging is a no-no.

Isolation is so over-rated in my opinion. If we were meant to be all alone, why did God put us in families? You see, family solves the issue of loneliness. And have you ever noticed that when you're alone, the enemy has so much more freedom and unmitigated nerve to use your mind as a playground?

When a predator is looking for food, they go after the weaker animal; the one that has strayed from the rest of the squad. This should tell us that we need each other for our greater good.

But the question is, in this world that puts emphasis on cutting everyone off, who is gonna be the one to say:

> "No! Stay and let's work things out!"

In a family where countless relatives are at odds with each other, who is going to be the one to leave their gift at the altar and go try to make it work?

I'm sick of going to funerals and seeing people performing out of guilt. I'm sick of losing people and asking myself "What could I have done better?"

Time is running out ya'll.

We need to be kinder to each other. We need to go the extra mile, we have to remember that what we are about to say out of strife could be our last exchange.

If you spend the majority of your time being angry at a loved one how many potential good times and memories are you missing out on right now?

Time is short. Life is but a vapor. Are you making your moments here count in the area of your relationships? All I'm saying is. . .

> Think twice before you decide to abandon that "family-ship."

READER'S NOTES . . .

1 Timothy 4:12 "Let no man despise thy youth; but be thou an example of the believers, in word, in conversation, in charity, in spirit, in faith, in purity."

YOUNG 'N BROKE

1 Timothy 4:12

It's 2019, and the struggle is real people! I see two disadvantages one can encounter in this day and age.

The first is being young. The second is being young with no money. How can I say this when our twenties are allegedly our so-called "best years?"

Well for one, when you're younger, it's harder to get employed. That's been my story, it's been my song. (And when we get a job it's not a quality one).

The ironic thing is, we need money to re-invent ourselves and to look good enough for corporate America. Or, we need money just to survive.

But HOW can we do that, if we keep getting rejected because of our age? This often happens because employers think that millennials or those in "Generation Y" don't take anything seriously, or they believe we are so problematic.

But in all honesty, both our generations are filled with very hard-working people. For a generation of people who aren't always taught life fundamentals in school, I think we do a darn good job.

We are often in college, trying to make a dollar out of fifteen cents, all because we lost a job opportunity to 45-year-old Susan, who doesn't want to relocate for work and who might not even appreciate the position once she gets it.

It is mighty funny how the people who refuse to pay us now, expect us to take care of them later. With the same money they didn't want to give us!!

I think it's time for us young 'n's to pave our own way if the corporate "they" won't give us a shot. If we use our gifts and talents relentlessly to invent things to solve the world's problems, we would never be broke again.

There's hope for us; we were created for something special. We will **not** just pay bills and then die.

No, we will push past this rough patch and change the game.

One talent at a time.

READER'S NOTES . . .

Proverbs 28:6 "Better is the poor that walketh in his uprightness, than he that is perverse in his ways, though he be rich."

POVERTY LINE

Proverbs 28:6

And since we are on the topic of finances, let me say a few more things.

No matter how high or low you fall on the poverty line, we all pretty much want the same things in life.

We want to be happy. We need to feel loved and appreciated, or even understood.

We want to be healthy and many of us want families.

With that being said, don't look down on someone because their cash flow doesn't match yours.

Also, please don't idolize a person who has money in abundance if you don't. Both sides need to leave the comparison game alone.

Why?

Because we all bleed red, and we all have a story to tell.

And when it's all said and done, we can't take our 50 cents or our $50 million with us. That should tell you that although money is important to get by in life, its importance is relative.

Whether you are well off or part of the "least of them,"

It shouldn't define who you are as a person either way.

READER'S NOTES . . .

Job 8:7 "Though thy beginning was small, yet thy latter end should greatly increase."

DEAR LITTLE CHELSEA

Job 8:7

Girl, there's so much I could tell you.

I know there are a lot of things you don't get right now. I know all about your pain, how you are so misunderstood, how you have big dreams. I have seen how people have tried to jade you, discouraging you from using your talents.

But just keep going, life really does get better, the bullies do shut up, you end up touching a lot of lives.

You will have degrees and diplomas in your name; you will discover your writing gift, and you'll come to see that there's so much life has to offer.

You will blossom into a better, more secure version of yourself. You will find your power to tear down the walls you've built up as a defense and/or coping mechanism.

And just know that I'm sorry for how hard I was on you. I should have never made you feel like you had to be perfect and without flaw, that's unrealistic.

But know that as an adult "You," I love you more than I ever thought I could have. And I really want you to know that it's okay. It really will be okay.

Golden Tones: Writing With Soul

If I could have a conversation with you face to face, I'd tell you that it's okay to be free and to be authentic. And that you weren't born to blend in anyways, so go ahead and become comfortable with being the beautiful, unique "oddball" that you are.

There's beauty in rarity.

READER'S NOTES . . .

Ephesians 6:4 "And, ye fathers, provoke not your children to wrath: but bring them up in the nurture and admonition of the Lord."

FATHER FAMINE

Ephesians 6:4

If fathers are present in the home, why are so many girls dealing with a father famine still? What could be so hard about loving and caring for the baby girl (or even baby boy) that **you** made?

How can you not be tempted to be part of everything? How can you not do surprise visits to your child's school to see how they are doing? How can you not show up to their games? How can you leave your daughter having to take her mom's brother to the father-daughter dance?

Having grandpa is nice, but it doesn't replace daddy.

And no: Mommy can't play both roles. The absence of daddy still pierces the heart. You are there without really being "there."

That's why there are so many girls having pregnancy scares in high school or who are looking for love in the wrong places.

They didn't mean to mess up or do the wrong thing. They just wanted male attention.

They keep trying to fill a hole that daddy left open. They can even fall victim to an abusive older man because he showed protective qualities in the beginning.

Qualities that "Daddy" should have instilled in them from the day they were born.

So just because your daughter says "That's okay Daddy, I'm sure you will make it next time," don't get it twisted. Her words are covering up the fact that she is hurt and may be scarred from your lack of attention.

It doesn't mean she feels whole or secure in the foundation that she has been given.

And when she angrily says "I don't need my daddy anyways!" don't think she's not fighting back the tears. Her tears may be the first wave of a tide that pushes her emotionally into the arms of a crowd who doesn't have her best interest at heart.

Fathers: before you choose not to take your relationship with your child to the next level, keep in mind that if you're not present whole heartedly for your own legacy. . .

> She will have to fight off a lot of devils.

READER'S NOTES . . .

2 Corinthians 10:12 "Not that we dare to classify or compare ourselves with some of those who are commending themselves. But when they measure themselves by one another and compare themselves with one another, they are without understanding."

COMPARISON IS A TOXIN

2 Corinthians 10:12

So what if you don't have a slim body like Stephanie, or a luxurious weave like Tanisha?

Comparison is a toxin.

You don't have one million followers like your frenemy, or a big house in Houston to rent like Tiffany? So what?

Comparison is a toxin.

So what if you're not engaged like Cassandra, or pregnant like Brittany? So what?

Comparison is a toxin.

Just because you don't have what someone else has doesn't mean you aren't doing well yourself. Even if they have what you want, exactly what you want, you don't know what dirty deed or what hardship they had to endure to get what they have now.

If you compare your blessings to theirs, keep it fair and also compare both your struggles. Since people only broadcast what they are proud of, you rarely see the entirety of their life. Think on this: behind closed doors their life may just be a hot mess.

That's why jealousy is silly. Learn to understand that timing and season is everything. What's for you will absolutely **not** pass you by.

Stop stressing yourself out and worrying so much. You have your own fingerprint in the world that can't be touched or duplicated.

Work with what you've got and receive the increase. When you're walking in your own destiny and truth, comparison will start to cease.

Nothing is wrong with you; you've been doing great all along. Always remember that just because their life is going one way. . .

Doesn't mean yours is wrong.

AUTHOR BIOGRAPHY

Chelsea G. Robinson is a graduate of Oakland Community College where she received her associate's degree in Performing Arts, focusing on theatre and music.

Her main goal in life is to change society and the generation she is a part of for the greater good. She values transparency and hopes to use her artistic expression in order to get her point across. "**Golden Tones: Writing With Soul**" is the first of Robinson's many writing ventures. She also enjoys writing about music and "real life" topics. Her passion is to help people think about why they do the things they do. She discovered this passion in college when she studied world religions, philosophy, and sociology.

Chelsea is a lover of life, God, family, and church. She currently attends and serves at Strong Tower Ministries, in Ypsilanti, Michigan. Her future plans include but are not limited to: producing music, acting, and encouraging the youth that cross her path to stay strong no matter what.

Follow Chelsea On her personal Facebook page:
Chelsea Glenn

www.ingramcontent.com/pod-product-compliance
Lightning Source LLC
Chambersburg PA
CBHW050637300426
44112CB00012B/1835